THIS BOOK
BELONGS TO

welcome to the world
a keepsake baby book

by Marfé Ferguson Delano

NATIONAL GEOGRAPHIC

Washington, D.C.

There Was a Child Went Forth.
by *Walt Whitman*

There was a child went forth every day,
And the first object he look'd upon, that
    object he became,
And that object became part of him for
    the day or a certain part of the day,
Or for many years or stretching cycles
    of years.

The early lilacs became part of this child,
And grass and white and red morning-
    glories, and white and red clover, and
    the song of the phoebe-bird,
And the Third-month lambs and the sow's
    pink-faint litter, and the mare's foal and the
    cow's calf,
And the noisy brood of the barnyard or by
    the mire of the pond-side,
And the fish suspending themselves so
    curiously below there, and the beautiful
    curious liquid,
And the water-plants with their graceful flat
    heads, all became part of him.

6

In a glittering galaxy swirling with stars...

On a beautiful blue planet called Earth...

Made of air and water...

And land and life...

YOU WERE BORN!

You arrived at _____

_____

_____.

You were delivered at _____

_____

by _____.

Your eyes were _____

_____

and your hair color was _____

_____.

You weighed _____

and measured _____.

{place photo here}

Welcome to the world!

{place photos here}

Our MEMORIES

of when you were born

_____
_____
_____
_____
_____
_____
_____
_____
_____
_____
_____

It's a world full of wonders,
    and it's waiting for you.

"This world is
but canvas to our
imaginations."
        —Henry David Thoreau

The Song of
the Stars

an Algonquian poem

We are the stars which sing,
We sing with our light;
We are the birds of fire,
We fly over the sky. . . .
We look down on the mountains.
This is the Song of the Stars.

"You are built not to shrink down to less, but to blossom into more. To be more splendid.

To be more extraordinary. To use every moment to fill yourself up."
—*Oprah Winfrey*

There's no one else exactly like you...

When you were born, we named you:

We chose this name because:

Other names we considered:

Sometimes we call you by other loving names. Here are some of your special nicknames:

Infant Joy
by William Blake

"I have no name:
"I am but two days old."
What shall I call thee?
"I happy am,
"Joy is my name."
Sweet joy befall thee!

Pretty joy!
Sweet joy but two days old,
Sweet joy I call thee:
Thou dost smile,
I sing the while,
Sweet joy befall thee!

And no other family is exactly like yours.

{place family photo here}

Family History

"Family members can be your best friends, you know.
And best friends, whether or not they are related to you, can be your family."
—*Trenton Lee Stewart*

_____
Me

_____   _____

_____   _____

_____   _____
Sisters   Brothers

_____
Mommy and Daddy

_____   _____

_____   _____
Maternal Grandparents   Paternal Grandparents

_____   _____

_____   _____
Great-Grandparents   Great-Grandparents

"Just where you are—that's the place to start."
—*Pema Chödrön*

From your very own home...

We brought you home to _____
_____

on _____
_____.

Here's how we got our home ready for you:

_____
_____
_____
_____
_____
_____
_____
_____
_____
_____

Your first visitors at home:

_____
_____
_____
_____
_____
_____
_____

"Ah! There is nothing like staying at home for real comfort."

—Jane Austen

To the neighborhood outside your door...

A few things about our neighborhood:

PLACE
STAMP HERE

To the big wide world beyond...
the possibilities are endless.

THE WORLD AS IT WAS WHEN YOU WERE Born

{Month/Day/Year}

WORLD HEADLINES

_____

OTHER PEOPLE IN THE NEWS

POLITICAL FIGURES

POPULAR SONGS

PRICE OF A GALLON OF MILK

PRICE OF A GALLON OF GASOLINE

"From wonder into wonder existence opens."

—*Lao-tzu*

From sunrise...

Morning memories: _____
_____
_____
_____
_____
_____
_____
_____
_____
_____
_____
_____
_____
_____

"Morning is when I am awake and there is dawn in me."
—*Henry David Thoreau*

To sunset...

Memories of watching a sunset with you: _____

_____

_____

_____

_____

_____

_____

_____

From sleepless nights...
    to quiet nights...it's a wonderful world.

"Oh sleep! it is a gentle thing,
Beloved from pole to pole!"
—*Samuel Taylor Coleridge*

The Land of Nod

by Robert Louis Stevenson

From breakfast on through all the day
At home among my friends I stay,
But every night I go abroad
Afar into the land of Nod.

All by myself I have to go,
With none to tell me what to do—
All alone beside the streams
And up the mountain-sides of dreams.

The strangest things are there for me,
Both things to eat and things to see,
And many frightening sights abroad
Till morning in the land of Nod.

Try as I like to find the way,
I never can get back by day,
Nor can remember plain and clear
The curious music that I hear.

When you started sleeping
through the night: _____
_____
_____
_____
_____
_____
_____
_____
_____
_____

Bedtime rituals: _____
_____
_____
_____
_____
_____
_____
_____

"Dreams come true; without that possibility,
nature would not incite us to have them."
—*John Updike*

It's a world to
dream
in...

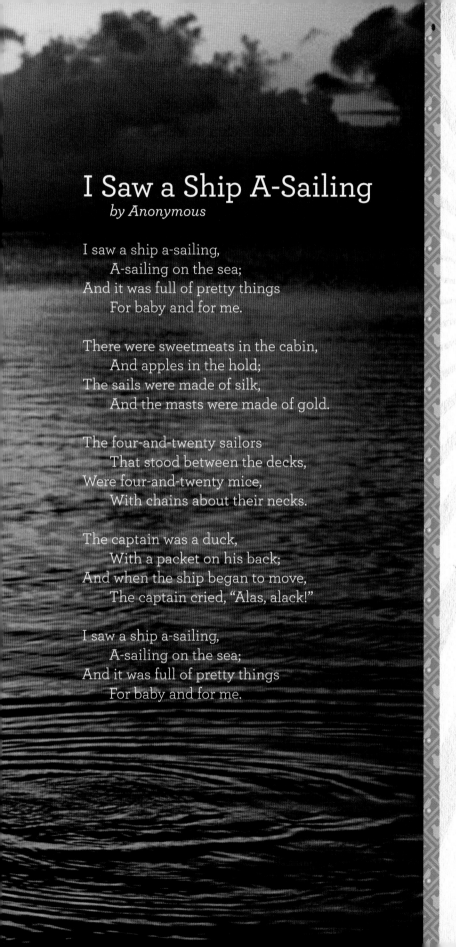

I Saw a Ship A-Sailing
by Anonymous

I saw a ship a-sailing,
    A-sailing on the sea;
And it was full of pretty things
    For baby and for me.

There were sweetmeats in the cabin,
    And apples in the hold;
The sails were made of silk,
    And the masts were made of gold.

The four-and-twenty sailors
    That stood between the decks,
Were four-and-twenty mice,
    With chains about their necks.

The captain was a duck,
    With a packet on his back;
And when the ship began to move,
    The captain cried, "Alas, alack!"

I saw a ship a-sailing,
    A-sailing on the sea;
And it was full of pretty things
    For baby and for me.

Our dreams for you: _____
_____
_____
_____
_____
_____
_____
_____
_____
_____
_____
_____
_____
_____
_____

To hope in...

Our hopes for you: _____

_____

_____

_____

_____

_____

_____

_____

_____

"Hope" is the thing with feathers –
by Emily Dickinson

"Hope" is the thing with feathers –
That perches in the soul –
And sings the tune without the words –
And never stops – at all –

And sweetest – in the Gale – is heard –
And sore must be the storm –
That could abash the little Bird
That kept so many warm –

I've heard it in the chillest land –
And on the strangest Sea –
Yet, never, in Extremity,
It asked a crumb – of Me.

"The sight of the stars always makes me dream."
—*Vincent Van Gogh*

Starlight,
Star Bright

*Mother Goose
nursery rhyme*

Starlight, star bright,
The first star
I see tonight,
I Wish I may,
I Wish I might,
Have this wish
I wish tonight.

"Growth itself contains the germ of happiness."

—*Pearl S. Buck*

Inch by inch...

day by day...month by month...

It's a world to sprout in, to bloom in...

"A single day is enough to make us a little larger."   —Paul Klee

57

To *bask* and **glow** and GROW in.

Height at birth: _____   Weight at birth: _____

AGE	HEIGHT	WEIGHT
1 week		
2 weeks		
1 month		
2 months		
3 months		
4 months		
6 months		
1 year		
2 years		
3 years		
4 years		
5 years		

{place photo here}

"Curiosity is, in great and generous minds,
the first passion and the last."
—*Samuel Johnson*

It's a world bursting with
tempting things to touch...

{place photo here}

When you first reached out and the things you reached for: _____

_____

_____

_____

_____

_____

_____

_____

_____

And taste...

"Bon appétit!"

—Julia Child

Your first tooth came in at age _____

You started eating solid foods at age _____.

Your favorite foods: _____

_____

_____

_____

Your least favorite foods: _____

_____

_____

_____

And *enjoy!*

When you first

Fed yourself: _____

_____

_____

Held a cup and drank from it: _____

_____

_____

Held a spoon: _____

_____

_____

Blueberries
by Robert Frost

"You ought to have seen what I saw on my way
To the village, through Patterson's pasture today:
Blueberries as big as the end of your thumb,
Real sky-blue, and heavy, and ready to drum
In the cavernous pail of the first one to come!
And all ripe together, not some of them green
And some of them ripe! You ought to have seen!"

"We begin to find and become ourselves when we notice how we are already found, already truly, entirely, wildly, messily, marvelously who we were born to be."

—Anne Lamott

Bold or bashful...Wild or tame...

"Against the assault of
laughter nothing
can stand."
—Mark Twain

When you first smiled:

When you first laughed:

Things that made you laugh:

You made people laugh when:

Things that made you mad or sad:

It's a world to be yourself in.

Unique things about your personality: _____

_____

_____

_____

_____

_____

_____

_____

_____

_____

_____

_____

_____

"Logic will get you from A to B. Imagination will take you everywhere." —*Albert Einstein*

"If you can't **fly**, run; if you can't run, walk; if you can't walk, **crawl**; but by all means keep *moving.*"

—Martin Luther King, Jr.

From tiny crawlers

to thundering herds...

From high flyers

to deep divers...

When you first...

Age

Rolled over _____

Sat up all by yourself _____

Crawled or crept _____

Took your first steps _____

Jumped _____

Danced _____

Ran _____

Skipped _____

Swam _____

Our memories of when you started to
crawl, walk, and more...

_____

_____

_____

_____

_____

_____

_____

_____

_____

Life
by Charlotte Brontë

Rapidly, merrily,
Life's sunny hours flit by,
Gratefully, cheerily,
Enjoy them as they fly!

It's a world to MOVE in, to SPLASH in, to SOAR and LEAP and DANCE in.

"Let us go singing as far as we go;
the road will be less tedious."

—*Virgil*

84

From whispering winds to crashing tides,

It's a world to listen in...

"How sweet the moonlight sleeps upon this bank!
Here will we sit and let the sounds of music
Creep in our ears. Soft stillness and the night
Become the touches of sweet harmony."

—William Shakespeare

A world to make
NOISE in...

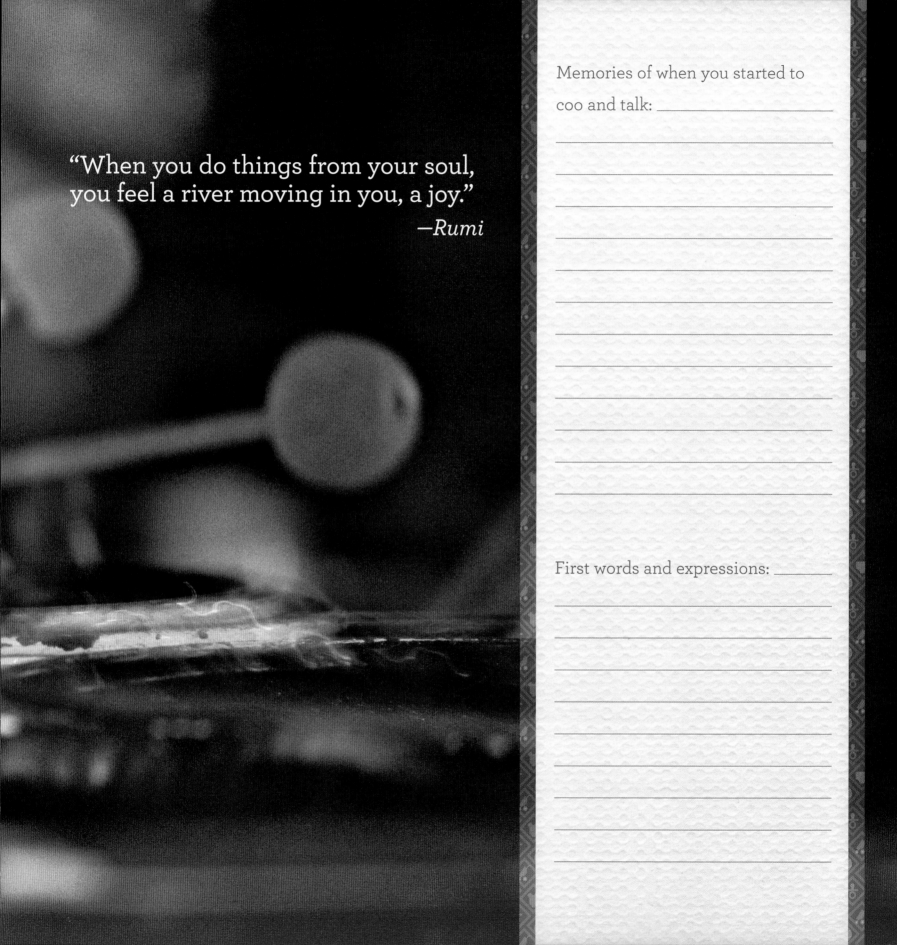

"When you do things from your soul,
you feel a river moving in you, a joy."

—*Rumi*

Memories of when you started to
coo and talk: _____
_____
_____
_____
_____
_____
_____
_____
_____
_____
_____
_____
_____

First words and expressions: _____
_____
_____
_____
_____
_____
_____
_____
_____
_____
_____

A world *humming* with song.

Your favorite lullabies and songs: _____

_____

_____

_____

_____

"The whole world seems
to smile upon me."
—*Samuel Pepys*

When you first sang: _____

_____

_____

_____

_____

"Surely all God's people, however serious and savage, great or small, like to play. Whales and elephants, dancing, humming gnats, and invisibly small mischievous microbes,—all are warm with divine radium and must have lots of fun in them."

—*John Muir*

It's a world to have *fun* in...

Your favorite games, books, and rhymes: _____

_____

_____

_____

_____

_____

_____

_____

_____

_____

_____

_____

"I never lose sight of the fact
that just being is fun."
–Katharine Hepburn

To spend time with friends in...

{place photo here}

Your favorite friends, pets, toys, and stuffed animals: _____

_____

_____

_____

_____

_____

_____

_____

"My friends have made the story of my life."
—Helen Keller

To kick up your heels in.

Girls and Boys, Come Out to Play

Mother Goose nursery rhyme

Girls and boys, come out to play,
The moon it shines as bright as day;
Leave your supper, and leave your sleep,
And come to your playmates in the street;
Come with a whoop, come with a call,
Come with a good will, or come not at all;
Up the ladder and down the wall,
A halfpenny loaf will serve us all.

"Be bold...When you
embark for strange places,
don't leave any of yourself
safely on shore."
—Alan Alda

"Look deep into nature, and then you will understand everything better."

—*Albert Einstein*

It's a world just *waiting* for you to explore.

The Explorer
by Rudyard Kipling

"Something hidden. Go and find it.
    Go and look behind the Ranges —
Something lost behind the Ranges.
    Lost and waiting for you. Go!"

Woods to wander...

Memories of exploring nature with you: _____

_____

_____

_____

_____

_____

_____

_____

_____

_____

Peaks to climb...

"In every walk with Nature
one receives far more
than he seeks."

—*John Muir*

Puddles to peer in...Tracks to trace.

"When you have seen one ant, one bird, one tree,
you have not seen them all."

—*Edward O. Wilson*

Blue evening falls,
Blue evening falls;
Nearby in every direction,
It sets the corn tassels trembling.

—From a Papago Indian song

"Adventure is worthwhile in itself."
—*Amelia Earhart*

So many adventures you'll have in this world!

Your first haircut:_____

_____

_____

_____

_____

Your first pet:_____

_____

_____

_____

{tape a lock of hair here}

Your first books:_____

_____

_____

Other memorable firsts: _____

_____

_____

_____

_____

_____

_____

You'll find paths to follow...

Family trips: _____

_____

_____

_____

_____

_____

113

And paths to blaze.

"All daring starts from within."
—Eudora Welty

How you showed your

independence: _____

_____

_____

_____

_____

_____

The Road Not Taken
by Robert Frost

Two roads diverged in a yellow wood,
And sorry I could not travel both
And be one traveler, long I stood
And looked down one as far as I could
To where it bent in the undergrowth;

Then took the other, as just as fair,
And having perhaps the better claim,
Because it was grassy and wanted wear;
Though as for that the passing there
Had worn them really about the same,

And both that morning equally lay
In leaves no step had trodden black.
Oh, I kept the first for another day!
Yet knowing how way leads on to way,
I doubted if I should ever come back.

I shall be telling this with a sigh
Somewhere ages and ages hence:
Two roads diverged in a wood, and I—
I took the one less traveled by,
And that has made all the difference.

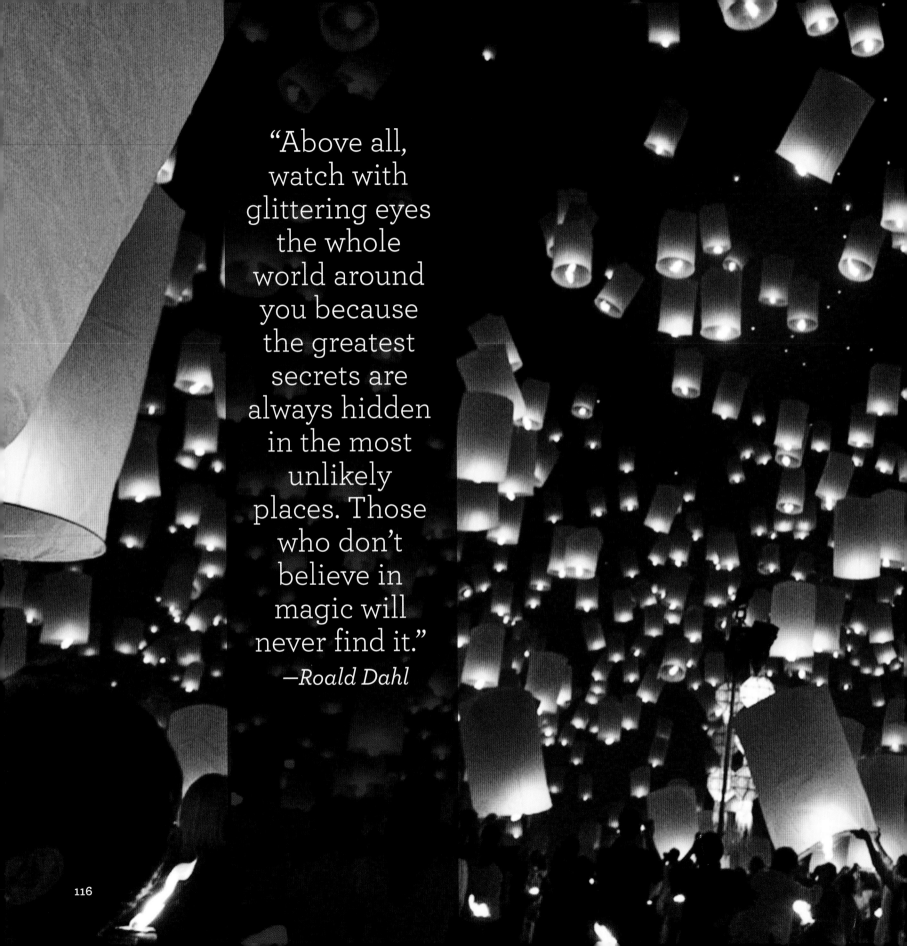

"Above all, watch with glittering eyes the whole world around you because the greatest secrets are always hidden in the most unlikely places. Those who don't believe in magic will never find it."
—*Roald Dahl*

116

And while you *discover* this wonderful world...

"Only those who risk going too far can possibly find out how far one can go."

—*T. S. Eliot*

As you search out its secrets and open your heart...

"Those who bring sunshine to the lives of others cannot keep it from themselves."
—*J. M. Barrie*

We'll learn new things too.

"Love isn't a state of perfect caring. It is an active noun like *struggle*. To love someone is to strive to accept that person exactly the way he or she is, right here and now."

—*Fred Rogers*

What we've learned from you: _____

_____

_____

_____

_____

_____

_____

_____

_____

_____

_____

_____

"Find out where *joy resides,* and give it a voice far beyond singing. For to miss the joy is *to miss all."*

—*Robert Louis Stevenson*

From your first birthday...

How we celebrated and what you did: _____

_____

_____

_____

_____

_____

_____

_____

_____

_____

_____

_____

_____

To special holidays...

There's so much to celebrate in this world!

What we are thankful for: _____

_____

_____

_____

_____

_____

_____

_____

_____

_____

"Every great dream begins with a dreamer. Always remember, you have within you the strength, the patience, and the passion to reach for the stars to change the world."

—*Harriet Tubman*

Reflections

on your first year

_____

_____

_____

_____

_____

_____

_____

_____

_____

_____

_____

_____

Reflections

on your second year

_____

_____

_____

_____

_____

_____

_____

_____

_____

_____

_____

_____

Reflections

on your third year

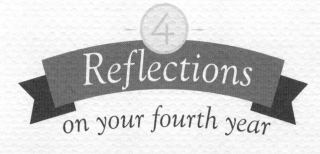

4 Reflections
on your fourth year

_____

_____

_____

_____

_____

_____

_____

_____

_____

_____

_____

_____

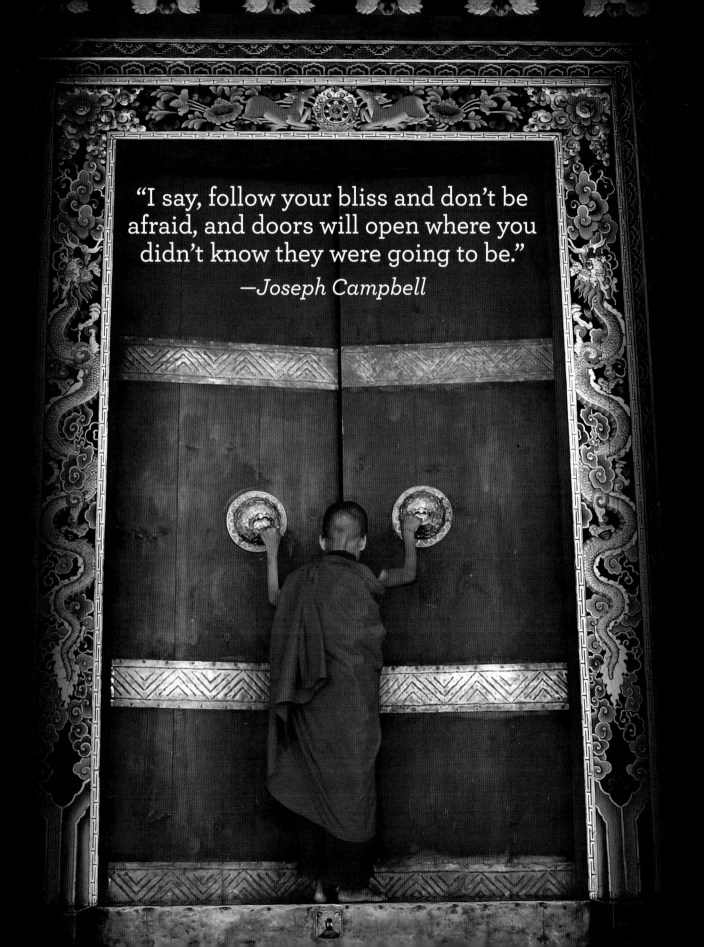

"I say, follow your bliss and don't be afraid, and doors will open where you didn't know they were going to be."
—*Joseph Campbell*

You're ready to blossom, to take off, to fly.

It's a wonderful world and it's waiting...

FOR You.

"Give to the world the best you have,
and the best will come back to you."
—*Madeline Bridges*

Time *never moves more quickly than it does while watching your* child grow.

As parents, we want to create a safe and healthy home, nurture and guide, and watch and learn as our baby navigates the wonders of our beautiful planet. To have a baby is to experience the utmost love and joy the world has to offer, while embracing the small moments, too—bath time, nighttime lullabies and cuddles, and new adventures are what make the early years special.

Welcome to the World creates a gorgeous space for preserving your baby's journey and cherishing the many firsts you will share together. Follow along as your child discovers life, laughter, and the people who love her. Celebrate as she takes her first steps, marvel as she says her first word, smile as she tastes her first foods, and—above all—be present so you can enjoy and remember each stage. There is a world of possibility and big dreams waiting, and you will have an unforgettable time exploring it together.

—*Jessica Alba, actress, activist, and co-founder of The Honest Company*

Index: *Milestones*

Photo Credits

NGYS = National Geographic Your Shot; SS = Shutterstock

Cover, Frans Lanting; Back cover, Lisa & Mike Husar/Team Husar; 1, Christie Kelsey/NGYS; 1, Miro Novak/SS; 2, happykanppy/SS; 3, Andy Rouse/naturepl.com; 4-5, Eiko Jones/NGYS; 6, NASA; 7, NASA; 8-9, NASA; 10-11, Callum Morse/NGYS; 12-13, Cesar Aristeiguieta/NGYS; 14, Fiona Rupert/NGYS; 16, happykanppy/SS; 18, Picsfive/SS; 19, Troy Lim/NGYS; 20-21, Lori Epstein/National Geographic Creative; 22, E+/Getty Images; 22 (Background), Jjustas/SS; 23, Flickr RF/Getty Images; 24, Martin Harvey/Workbook Stock/Getty Images; 25, Shmeliova Natalia/SS; 26-27, Jane Bullard/NGYS; 28, Ronan Donovan/NGYS; 29, happykanppy/SS; 31, ZSSD/Minden Pictures; 32, Jiri Vaclavek/SS; 32-33, Steve Elms/NGYS; 34, diez artwork/SS; 35, Sebastian Wasek/NGYS; 36-37, Andrey Antov/NGYS; 38-39, Christos Tsoumplekas/NGYS; 40-41, Alicia Herrera Ulibarri/NGYS; 42-43, Norbert Rosing/

National Geographic Creative; 44-45, Chiu Fung Wong/NGYS; 46-47, Mark Lewis/Stone Sub/Getty Images; 47 (Background), pashabo/SS; 48-49, Navid Baraty/NGYS; 49, Miro Novak/SS; 50-51, Stian Klo/NGYS; 52-53, Jason Ward/NGYS; 54-55, Juan Pablo Soto/NGYS; 56, Lemuel Ollet/NGYS; 57, Thomas Peck/Millennium Images, UK; 59, Digital Vision/Photodisc/Getty Images; 60-61, Diane Kostan/NGYS; 62, Roxi Mueller/NGYS; 63, Miro Novak/SS; 64, Christian Stepien/NGYS; 65, happykanppy/SS; 65, Sergey Peterman/SS; 66, Lim Yong Hian/SS; 67, B. and E. Dudzinscy/SS; 68-69, Todd Davis/NGYS; 70, Miro Novak/SS; 70, James Goulding/NGYS; 71, Jonathan Garcia/NGYS; 72, Miro Novak/SS; 72, Tc Morgan/NGYS; 74, Miro Novak/SS; 74-75, Cheryl McMahan/NGYS; 75, pashabo/SS; 76, Scott Stonum/NGYS; 78, Mehmet Karaca/NGYS; 79, Nick Cordrey/NGYS; 80, Josh Hed/NGYS;

Index: *Authors and Poems*

Poetry and Quotation Sources

There Was a Child Went Forth., Walt Whitman. From *Leaves of Grass*.

"This world..." Henry David Thoreau. From *A Week on the Concord and Merrimack Rivers*.

The Song of the Stars, an Algonquian poem. Available in *The Classic Treasury of Childhood Wonders* by Susan Magsamen. Washington, D.C.: National Geographic Society, 2010.

"You are built not to shrink down to less..." Oprah Winfrey

Infant Joy, William Blake. From *Songs of Innocence and Experience*.

"Family members can be..." Trenton Lee Stewart. From *The Mysterious Benedict Society*. New York: Little, Brown and Company, 2008. Used by permission of Hachette Book Group.

"Just where you are..." Pema Chödrön. From *Comfortable With Uncertainty*. Boston, MA: Shambhala Publications, 2003.

"Ah! There is nothing..." Jane Austen. From *Emma*.

"From wonder..." Lao-tzu. From *Tao Te Ching*.

"Morning is..." Henry David Thoreau. From *Walden*.

"Oh sleep!..." Samuel Taylor Coleridge. From *The Rime of the Ancient Mariner*.

The Land of Nod, Robert Louis Stevenson. From *A Child's Garden of Verses*.

"Dreams come true..." John Updike. From *Getting the Words Out*. Northridge, CA: Lord John Press, 1988.

I Saw a Ship A-Sailing, Anonymous. Available in *Leave Your Sleep: A Collection of Classic Children's Poetry*, by Natalie Merchant and Barbara McClintock. New York: Farrar, Straus and Giroux, 2012.

"Hope" is the thing with feathers, Emily Dickinson. From *The Poems of Emily Dickinson: Variorum Edition,* edited by Ralph W. Franklin. Cambridge, MA: The Belknap Press of Harvard University Press, 1998. Copyright © 1998 by the President and Fellows of Harvard College. Copyright © 1951, 1955, 1979, 1983 by the President and Fellows of Harvard College.

"The sight of the stars..." Vincent van Gogh. In a letter to his brother Theo, quoted in *Van Gogh and the Colors of the Night*, by Sjraar van Heugten, et al., trans. Lynne Richards. Museum of Modern Art: New York, 2008.

Starlight, Star Bright, Mother Goose nursery rhyme. Available in *The Classic Treasury of Childhood Wonders*.

"Growth itself contains..." Pearl S. Buck. From *To My Daughters, With Love*.

"A single day..." Paul Klee. From *The Diaries of Paul Klee 1898–1918*. Berkeley and Los Angeles, CA: University of California Press, 1968.

"Curiosity is..." Samuel Johnson. From *The Rambler* no. 150.

"Bon appétit!" Julia Child

"Fingers were made..." Jonathan Swift. From *Polite Conversation*.

Blueberries, Robert Frost. From *Robert Frost Selected Poems*. New York: Gramercy Books, 2001.

"We begin to find..." Anne Lamott. From "Becoming the Person You Were Meant to Be." Originally published in *O, the Oprah magazine*. Copyright © 2009 by Anne Lamott, used by permission of The Wylie Agency LLC. www.oprah.com/spirit/How-To-Find-Out-Who-You-Really-Are-by-Anne-Lamott

"Against the assault of laughter..." Mark Twain. From *The Mysterious Stranger*.

"Logic will get you..." Albert Einstein

"If you can't fly, run…" Martin Luther King, Jr. From an address given on Founders Day at Spelman College, April 11, 1960. © 1960 Dr. Martin Luther King, Jr. © renewed 1988 Coretta Scott King. www5 .spelman.edu/about_us/news/ pdf/70622_messenger.pdf

Life, Charlotte Brontë. From *The Life and Works of Charlotte Brontë and Her Sisters.*

"Let us go singing…" Virgil. From *The Ecologues.*

"How sweet the moonlight sleeps…" William Shakespeare. From *The Merchant of Venice.*

"When you do things from your soul…" Rumi. From *The Soul of Rumi,* trans. Coleman Barks. New York: Harper Collins, 2000.

"The whole world seems to smile upon me." Samuel Pepys. From *The Diary of Samuel Pepys* (October 31, 1662, entry).

"Surely all God's people…" John Muir. From *The Story of My Boyhood and Youth.*

"I never lose sight…" Katharine Hepburn

"My friends have made…" Helen Keller. From *The Story of My Life.*

Girls and Boys, Come Out to Play, Mother Goose nursery rhyme. From *Mother Goose or the Old Nursery Rhymes.*

"Be bold…" Alan Alda. From *Things I Overheard While Talking to Myself.* New York: Random House, 2007.

"Look deep into nature…" Albert Einstein

The Explorer, Rudyard Kipling. From *Collected Verse of Rudyard Kipling.*

"In every walk…" John Muir. From *Steep Trails.*

"When you have seen one ant…" Edward O. Wilson. From "The Quiet Apocalypse." *Time,* October 13, 1986.

"Blue evening falls," Papago Indian song. Available in *Winged Serpent: American Indian Prose and Poetry,* ed. Margot Astrov.

"Adventure is…" Amelia Earhart. Amelia Earhart™ is a trademark of Amy Kleppner, as heir to the Estate of Muriel Morrissey. www .AmeliaEarhart.com

"All daring…" Eudora Welty. Reprinted by permission of the publisher from *One Writer's Beginnings,* by Eudora Welty, p. 104. Cambridge, MA: Harvard University Press. Copyright © 1983, 1984 by Eudora Welty.

The Road Not Taken, Robert Frost. From *Robert Frost Selected Poems.*

"Above all…" Roald Dahl. From *The Minpins.*

"Only those who risk going too far…" T. S. Eliot

"Those who bring sunshine…" J. M. Barrie. From *A Window in Thrums.*

"Love isn't a state…" Fred Rogers. From *The World According to Mr. Rogers, Important Things to Remember.* New York: Hyperion, 2003. Used by permission of Hachette Book Group.

"Find out where joy resides…" Robert Louis Stevenson. From "The Lantern-Bearers," in *The Lantern-Bearers and Other Essays.* New York: Cooper Square Press, 1999.

"Every great dream begins with a dreamer…" Harriet Tubman

"I say, follow your bliss…" Joseph Campbell. From *The Power of Myth.* New York: Doubleday, 1988.

"Give to the world the best…" Madeline Bridges. From "Life's Mirror," in *Poems That Touch the Heart,* compiled by A. L. Alexander. New York: Doubleday, 1941.

Published by the National Geographic Society
John M. Fahey, *Chairman of the Board and Chief Executive Officer*
Declan Moore, *Executive Vice President; President,*
    Publishing and Travel
Melina Gerosa Bellows, *Executive Vice President; Chief Creative*
    Officer, Books, Kids, and Family

Prepared by the Book Division
Hector Sierra, *Senior Vice President and General Manager*
Nancy Laties Feresten, *Senior Vice President, Kids Publishing*
    and Media
Jennifer Emmett, *Vice President, Editorial Director,*
    Children's Books
Eva Absher-Schantz, *Design Director, Kids Publishing and Media*
Jay Sumner, *Director of Photography, Kids Publishing and Media*
R. Gary Colbert, *Production Director*
Jennifer A. Thornton, *Director of Managing Editorial*

Staff for This Book
Jennifer Emmett, *Project Editor*
Eva Absher-Schantz, *Art Director and Designer*
Lori Epstein, *Senior Photo Editor*
Ariane Szu-Tu, *Editorial Assistant*
Callie Broaddus, *Design Production Assistant*
Margaret Leist, *Photo Assistant*
Grace Hill, *Associate Managing Editor*
Joan Gossett, Michael O'Connor, *Production Editors*
Lewis R. Bassford, *Production Manager*
Susan Borke, *Legal and Business Affairs*
Paige Towler, *Editorial Intern*

Production Services
Phillip L. Schlosser, *Senior Vice President*
Chris Brown, *Vice President, NG Book Manufacturing*
George Bounelis, *Senior Production Manager*
Nicole Elliott, *Director of Production*
Rachel Faulise, *Manager*
Robert L. Barr, *Manager*

The publisher gratefully acknowledges the efforts of Natalie
Turner in securing permissions.

The National Geographic Society is one of the world's largest
nonprofit scientific and educational organizations. Founded
in 1888 to "increase and diffuse geographic knowledge," the
Society's mission is to inspire people to care about the planet.
It reaches more than 400 million people worldwide each month
through its official journal, *National Geographic*, and other
magazines; National Geographic Channel; television documen-
taries; music; radio; films; books; DVDs; maps; exhibitions; live
events; school publishing programs; interactive media; and
merchandise. National Geographic has funded more than 10,000
scientific research, conservation and exploration projects and
supports an education program promoting geographic literacy.

For more information, please visit www.nationalgeographic.com,
call 1-800-NGS LINE (647-5463), or write to the following address:

National Geographic Society
1145 17th Street N.W.
Washington, D.C. 20036-4688 U.S.A.

Visit us online at www.nationalgeographic.com/books

For librarians and teachers:
www.ngchildrensbooks.org

More for kids from National Geographic:
kids.nationalgeographic.com

For information about special discounts for bulk purchases,
please contact National Geographic Books Special Sales:
ngspecsales@ngs.org

For rights or permissions inquiries, please contact National
Geographic Books Subsidiary Rights: ngbookrights@ngs.org

ISBN: 978-1-4262-1314-4

Printed in China

14/RRDS/1